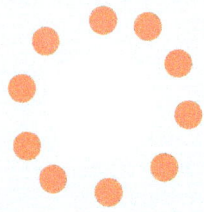

This book belongs to

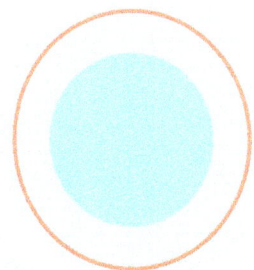

Mummy's family

_____
Great grandfather

_____
Great grandmother

_____
Grandfather

_____
Grandmother

_____
Mummy

_____
Mummy's siblings

_____
Mummy's siblings

_____
Mummy's siblings

_____
Mummy's siblings

_____
My cousins

_____
My cousins

_____
My cousins

_____
My cousins

_____
My cousins

_____
My cousins

Daddy's family

_____
Great grandfather

_____
Great grandmother

_____
Grandfather

_____
Grandmother

_____
Daddy

_____
Daddy's siblings

_____
Daddy's siblings

_____
Daddy's siblings

_____
Daddy's siblings

_____
My cousins

_____
My cousins

_____
My cousins

_____
My cousins

_____
My cousins

_____
My cousins

Mummy and daddy

A picture of mummy and daddy

How we met_____

_____

Our favourite memory together_____

_____

The funniest thing we went through together_____

_____

My family

A picture of my family

I have _____ brothers _____ and sisters.

Their names and ages are_____

_____

_____

_____

_____

Before I was born

Mummy first found out she was pregnant when I was_____

What mummy loved to eat while pregnant _____

_____

The first time mummy felt me move _____

While pregnant mummy gained _____

Mummy and daddy's most favourite memories during pregnancy

_____

_____

_____

_____

_____

_____

_____

_____

Before I was born

Place ultrasound photo here

Date _____

Thoughts _____

_____

_____

_____

Before I was born

A photo of mummy while pregnant

Date _____

ووَصَّيْنَا الإِنسَانَ بِوَالِدَيْهِ إِحْسَاناً
حَمَلَتْهُ أُمُّهُ كُرْهاً وَوَضَعَتْهُ كُرْهاً.

And We have enjoined upon man, to his parents,
good treatment. His mother carried him with
hardship and gave birth to him with hardship.
The Holy Quran, chapter 46 verse 15

Before I was born

A photo of mummy while pregnant

Mummy's thoughts while pregnant —————————————————————

——

——

——

——

A letter from mummy

A letter from daddy

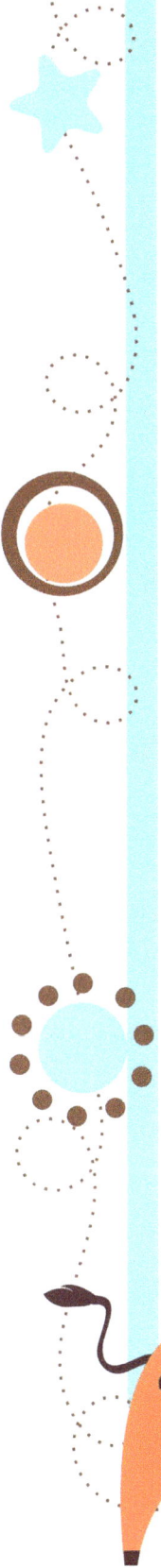

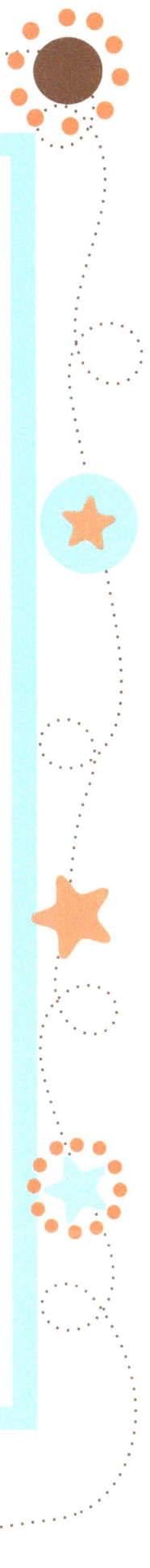

My arrival

How I was delivered _____

The doctor who delivered me _____

Place of delivery _____

Time of delivery _____

The first person to carry me _____

The person who cut my umbilical cord_____

The people present on that day_____

_____

_____

_____

My special characteristics_____

_____

_____

_____

_____

My arrival

The first real picture of me

للّه مُلْكُ السَّمٰوَاتِ وَالأَرْض يَخْلُقُ مَا يَشَاءُ
يَهَبُ لِمَنْ يَشَاءُ إِنَاثاً وَيَهَبُ لِمَنْ يَشَاءُ الذُّكُورَ

To Allah belongs the dominion of the heavens
and the earth; He creates what he wills. He
gives to whom He wills female [children], and
He gives to whom He wills males.
The Holy Quran, chapter 42 verse 49

My arrival

My name is _____

My family chose this special name because _____

_____

The meaning of my name is _____

_____

ذكر أبو داود في السنن عن أبي الدرداء : أن رسول الله صلى الله عليه وسلم قال :

إنكم تدعون يوم القيامة بأسمائكم وأسماء آبائكم

فحسنوا أسماءكم

It was narrated that the prophet (pbuh) said: You will be called on the Judgement day by your names and your fathers' names so choose for yourselves good names.

Narrated by Abu Dawood, Hassan

My arrival

My tiny handprint

My tiny footprint

My arrival

A photo of me and mummy

Date _____

Thoughts _____

_____

_____

_____

My arrival

A photo of me and daddy

Date _____

Thoughts _____

_____

_____

_____

Welcome home

I came home when I was _____ weeks old.

The address of my first home was _____

_____

I was welcomed at home by _____

_____

What I did the first week at home _____

_____

_____

_____

_____

_____

وَإِنْ تَعُدُّوا نِعْمَةَ اللَّهِ لَا تُحْصُوهَا إِنَّ اللَّهَ لَغَفُورٌ رَحِيمٌ

And if you should count the favors of Allah , you could not enumerate them. Indeed, Allah is Forgiving and Merciful.

The Holy Quran, chapter 16 verse 18

Welcome home

Place photo here

Place photo here

Welcome home

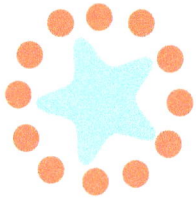

Place photo here

Place photo here

Welcome home

Place photo here

Place photo here

My Aqeeqah

Place photo here

Date _____

People present on that day _____

_____

_____

_____

_____

_____

_____

My Aqeeqah

عَنْ مُحَمَّدِ بْنِ سِيرِينَ حَدَّثَنَا سَلْمَانُ بْنُ عَامِرٍ الضَّبِّىُّ قَالَ سَمِعْتُ رَسُولَ اللَّهِ صلى الله عليه وسلم يَقُولُ مَعَ الْغُلاَمِ عَقِيقَةٌ ، فَأَهْرِيقُوا عَنْهُ دَمًا وَأَمِيطُوا عَنْهُ الأَذَى.

Narrated By Salman bin 'Amir Ad-Dabbi : I heard Allah's Apostle (pbuh) saying, "'Aqeeqah is to be offered for a newly born, so slaughter (an animal) for him, and relieve him of his suffering." Related by Saheeh Bukhari

Thoughts on that day _____

_____

_____

_____

_____

_____

_____

_____

Watch me grow

Date	Age	Weight	Height
_____	1 month	_____	_____
_____	2 months	_____	_____
_____	3 months	_____	_____
_____	4 month	_____	_____
_____	5 months	_____	_____
_____	6 months	_____	_____
_____	7 month	_____	_____
_____	8 months	_____	_____
_____	9 months	_____	_____
_____	10 month	_____	_____
_____	11 months	_____	_____
_____	12 months	_____	_____

Watch me grow

My blood type is _____

My first visits to the doctor _____

_____

_____

_____

_____

ثُمَّ خَلَقْنَا النُّطْفَةَ عَلَقَةً فَخَلَقْنَا الْعَلَقَةَ مُضْغَةً فَخَلَقْنَا الْمُضْغَةَ عِظَاماً فَكَسَوْنَا الْعِظَامَ لَحْماً ثُمَّ أَنشَأْنَاهُ خَلْقاً آخَرَ فَتَبَارَكَ اللَّهُ أَحْسَنُ الْخَالِقِينَ.

Then We made the sperm-drop into a clinging clot, and We made the clot into a lump [of flesh], and We made [from] the lump, bones, and We covered the bones with flesh; then We developed him into another creation. So blessed is Allah , the best of creators. The Holy Quran, chapter 23 verse 14

Watch me grow

I first had solid foods was when I was _____ old.

My favourite foods were _____

_____

_____

I first fed myself when I was _____ old.

What mummy and daddy did to get me to eat my food _____

_____

_____

_____

_____

Foods I didn't really like _____

_____

_____

_____

_____

_____

Watch me grow

A picture of me eating

Some funny memories of me with my food_____

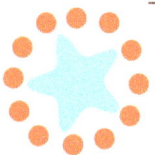

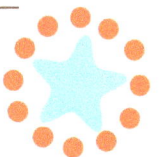

_____

_____

_____

_____

_____

_____

Watch me grow

A picture of me sleeping

I used to wake up _____times a night.

I first slept through the night when I was_____ old.

Thoughts of mummy and daddy when they see me sleeping_____

_____

_____

_____

Watch me grow

M   D   Y   M   D   Y
1. ___/___/___   ___/___/___ .1
2. ___/___/___   ___/___/___ .2
3. ___/___/___   ___/___/___ .3
4. ___/___/___   ___/___/___ .4
5. ___/___/___   ___/___/___ .5
6. ___/___/___   ___/___/___ .6

6. ___/___/___   ___/___/___ .6
5. ___/___/___   ___/___/___ .5
4. ___/___/___   ___/___/___ .4
3. ___/___/___   ___/___/___ .3
2. ___/___/___   ___/___/___ .2
1. ___/___/___   ___/___/___ .1

My first tooth appeared when I was_____old.

What I was like when I got new teeth_____

_____

_____

_____

My first hair cut

Before

After

Me in the bath

A photo of me in the bath

Date _____

Thoughts _____

_____

_____

_____

Watch me grow

I first smiled when I was_____ old.

The first person I smiled at was_____

I first rolled over when I was_____ old.

The first time I sat by myself I was_____ old.

I first crawled when I was_____ old.

I first stood up by myself when I was_____ old.

The first time I blew a kiss I was_____ old.

The first person I kissed was_____

My first time to walk was when I was_____old.

I first spoke when I was_____old.

Some of my first words were_____

_____

_____

_____

_____

Watch me grow

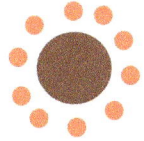

Place photo here

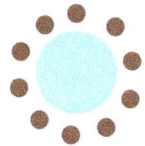

Place photo here

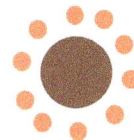

 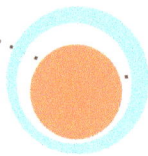  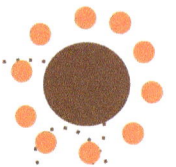

Watch me grow

My favourite colour was _____

My favourite toys were _____

_____

Some of the books I loved to read _____

_____

_____

Some of the things I loved to do _____

_____

_____

_____

_____

My favourite trips outside _____

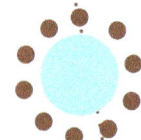

_____

_____

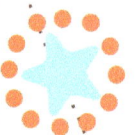

_____

_____

_____

Watch me grow

Place photo here

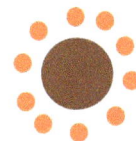

Place photo here

My first time in a mosque

Place photo here

Date_____

Mummy and daddy's thoughts_____

_____

_____

_____

_____

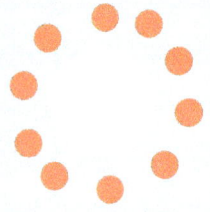

My first time in a mosque

إنما يعمر مساجد الله من آمن بالله واليوم الآخر وأقام الصلاة وآتى الزكاة ولم يخش إلا الله فعسى أولئك أن يكونوا من المهتدين.

The mosques of Allah are only to be maintained by those who believe in Allah and the Last Day and establish prayer and give zakah and do not fear except Allah , for it is expected that those will be of the [rightly] guided.

The Holy Quran, chapter 9 verse 18

Mummy and daddy's advice to me _____

_____

_____

_____

_____

Watch me grow

Date	Age	Weight	Height
_____	18 months	_____	_____
_____	24 months	_____	_____
_____	2.5 years	_____	_____
_____	3 years	_____	_____
_____	3.5 years	_____	_____
_____	4 years	_____	_____
_____	4.5 years	_____	_____
_____	5 years	_____	_____
_____	5.5 years	_____	_____
_____	6 years	_____	_____
_____	6.5 years	_____	_____
_____	7 years	_____	_____

Watch me grow

The first chapter I learnt of the Quran was _____

I first completed a juz' of the Quran when I was _____

The first prophetic hadith I learnt was _____

_____

Mummy and daddy's advice to me _____

_____

_____

وَقُلْ رَبِّ زِدْنِي عِلْمًا.

And say, "My Lord, increase me in knowledge."
The Holy Quran, chapter 20 verse 114

My first Ramadan

Place photo here

I first spent Ramadan with my family when I was —————— old.

شَهْرُ رَمَضَانَ الَّذِي أُنزِلَ فِيهِ الْقُرْآنُ هُدًى لِّلنَّاسِ وَبِينَاتٍ مِّنَ الْهُدَى وَالْفُرْقَانِ.

The month of Ramadhan [is that] in which was revealed the Qur'an, a guidance for the people and clear proofs of guidance and criterion.

The Holy Quran chapter 2 verse 185

First time to fast Ramadan

Place photo here

I first fasted Ramadan when I was_____ old.

Thoughts _____

_____

_____

_____

_____

_____

_____

My first eid fitr

Place photo here

Date _____

Thoughts _____

_____

_____

_____

My first eid adha

Place photo here

Date _____

Thoughts _____

_____

_____

_____

My first time to pray

Place photo here

Date_____

Mummy and daddy's thoughts_____

_____

_____

_____

_____

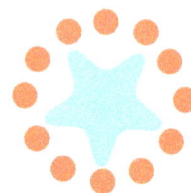

My first time to pray

حَافِظُوا عَلَى الصَّلَوَاتِ وَالصَّلَاةِ الْوُسْطَى وَقُومُوا لِلَّهِ قَانِتِينَ.

Maintain with care the [obligatory] prayers and [in particular] the middle prayer and stand before Allah , devoutly obedient.

The Holy Quran, chapter 2 verse 238

Mummy and daddy's advice to me _____

_____

_____

_____

_____

One year old today

Place photo here

Things I achieved this year_____
_____
_____

Mummy and daddy's thoughts_____
_____
_____
_____

Two years old today

Place photo here

Things I achieved this year _____
_____
_____

Mummy and daddy's thoughts _____
_____
_____

Three years old today

Place photo here

Things I achieved this year _____

_____

_____

_____

Mummy and daddy's thoughts _____

_____

_____

_____

Four years old today

Place photo here

Things I achieved this year _____

_____

_____

_____

Mummy and daddy's thoughts _____

_____

_____

_____

My first day of school

I first started school when I was _____ years old.

My first day of school was _____

The colour of my school uniform was _____

I was really excited because _____

_____

What I loved most about school _____

_____

_____

_____

Mummy and daddy's thoughts _____

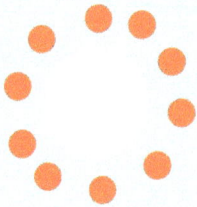

_____

_____

_____

_____

My first day of school

Place photo here

Place photo here

Special memories

Place photo here

Thoughts _____

_____

_____

_____

_____

_____

_____

_____

Special memories

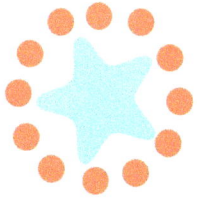

Place photo here

Place photo here

Special memories

Place photo here

Thoughts _____

_____

_____

_____

_____

Special memories

Place photo here

Place photo here

Special memories

Place photo here

Thoughts _____
_____
_____
_____
_____

Special memories

Place photo here

Place photo here

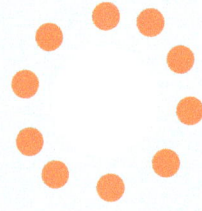

وَقَالَ رَبِّ أَوْزِعْنِي أَنْ أَشْكُرَ نِعْمَتَكَ الَّتِي أَنْعَمْتَ عَلَيَّ وَعَلَى وَالِدَيَّ وَأَنْ أَعْمَلَ صَالِحاً تَرْضَاهُ

My Lord, enable me to be grateful for

Your favor which You have bestowed upon

me and upon my parents and to work

righteousness of which You will approve

The holy Quran 46:15

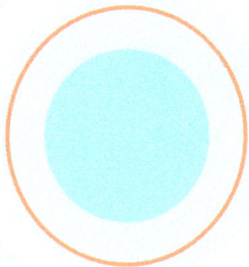

Halah Azim
Baby boy - A gift from Allah

© 2013, Halah Azim
www.theheartsoflight.com

To get more unique Islamic products for the whole family visit: www.theheartsoflight.com
and make sure to join us on facebook, www.facebook.com/TheHeartsOfLight

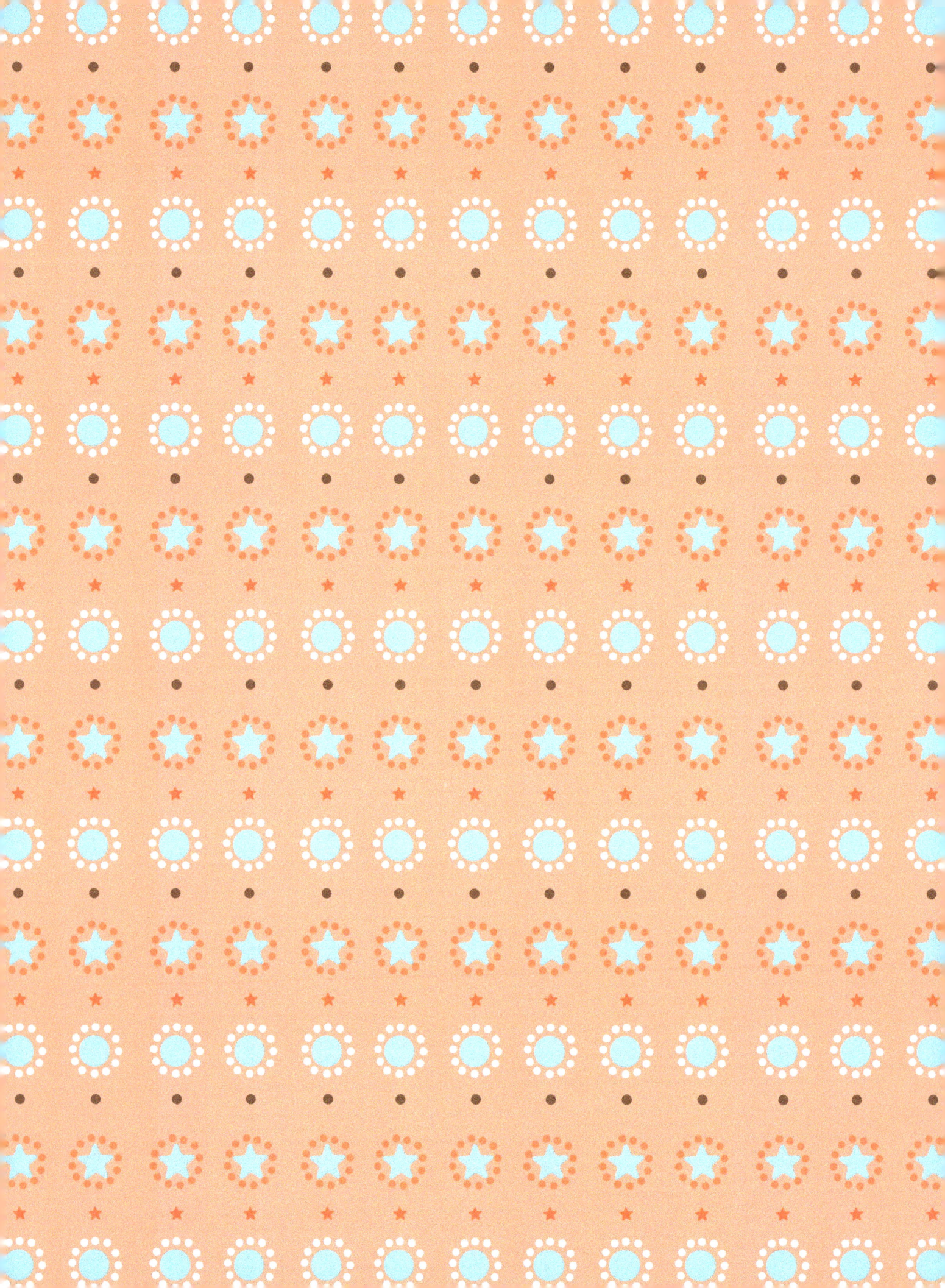